HEATHCLIFF
CATCH OF THE DAY

The funniest feline in America delights millions of fans every day as he appears in over 500 newspapers. You'll have a laugh a minute as Heathcliff tangles with the milkman, the mailman, the veterinarian and just about everyone else he runs into. If you're looking for some fun, look no further. Heathcliff is here!

HEATHCLIFF®
CATCH OF THE DAY

by
Geo Gately

C
CHARTER BOOKS, NEW YORK

Cartoons previously published in
Heathcliff Banquet

HEATHCLIFF CATCH OF THE DAY

A Charter Book / published by arrangement with
McNaught Syndicate, Inc.

PRINTING HISTORY
Charter edition / February 1986

ISBN: 0-441-32237-9

Charter Books are published by The Berkley Publishing Group,
200 Madison Avenue, New York, New York 10016.
PRINTED IN THE UNITED STATES OF AMERICA

"HEATHCLIFF!...DON'T DO IT!!"

"YOU'LL HAVE TO BE PATIENT UNTIL WE GET TO THE WISHBONE."

"STRANGE!...THAT'S THE ONLY PATCH OF ICE IN TOWN!"

"HE JUST TORE THE HIDE OFF OF THAT SHEEPDOG!"

"FOR SOME REASON, HE SEEMS TO FIND
MY HAIRCUTS AMUSING."

"HEATHCLIFF!!...."

© 1975
McNaught Synd., Inc.

1-28

"ARE YOU TRYING TO TELL ME HEATHCLIFF
WENT AFTER A SAINT BERNARD?!"

"SOMEBODY SLIPPED A TEN DOLLAR BILL IN MY POCKET!"

"HAH! FINALLY CAUGHT YA WITHOUT THAT DUMB CAT!"

"GESUNDHEIT!"

"YOU NEVER KNOW. SOMEDAY, YOU MAY NEED OUR SERVICES."

" CATNIP AND ROSES. "

"SPIKE!—WHAT HAPPENED TO YOUR COSTUME?!"

"TRICK OR TREAT!"

"I KNOW THE LAWN NEEDS RAKING!"

"KEEP OUR MASCOT AWAY FROM THE TACKLING DUMMY!"

"THEY'RE PICKING OUT A HALLOWEEN COSTUME!"

"FINISHED WITH YOUR SCRATCHING POST, HONEYBUN?"

"MASCOTS DO NOT BLOCK FIELD GOALS!"

"HEATHCLIFF WOULDN'T PLAY DOLL CARRIAGE, SO I THOUGHT I'D MAKE HIM JEALOUS WITH CHAUNCY!"

"YESIREE, FOLKS....THREE OUT OF FOUR CATS PREFER 'LIVER LUMPS'!"

"OH, DEAR!... MY SLIP IS SHOWING!"

"TO MR. HEATHCLIFF NUTMEG...'DEAR SIR, I'M SORRY
YOU DON'T FEEL PROPERLY REPRESENTED...!'"

"THERE'S NOTHING WRONG WITH YOUR ARCH!"

"I THINK YOUR LIGHT IS DISTURBING HIM."

"HE'S VERY TICKLISH!"

"HE ENJOYS A FAMILY STYLE RESTAURANT."

"HE'S GOT AN ACCOMPLICE!"

"I WISH YOU'D LEARN TO RING THE DOORBELL!"

"...AND HERE WE HAVE YOUR SIGNED CONFESSION!"

"HE'S GOT A VERY BUSY DAY, TOMORROW."

"NICE TACKLE!"

"HAS ANYONE SEEN MY HAIR DRYER?"

"PLEASE, HEATHCLIFF! YOU'VE GOT TO LOSE SOME WEIGHT...
...TRY THIS TUNA FLAVORED YOGURT."

"HE WON'T ENTER IF HE DOESN'T LIKE THE TROPHIES."

"AH, GOOD!...NO SIGN OF HEATHCLIFF!"

"ONE WAY OR ANOTHER, HE ALWAYS CATCHES THEM!"

"ACCORDING TO THIS, ONE OF THE SHIPS
IN THE TUNA FLEET WENT DOWN."

"NOT MANY COUPLES SHOWED UP FOR THE HAYRIDE!"

"NOW, YOU WERE COMING UP THE WALK, DELIVERING THE MILK... AND THEN WHAT HAPPENED?"

"WHO'S THE LITTLE GUY IN THE CAT COSTUME?"

"NO, NO, HEATHCLIFF!...BE A GOOD SPORT ABOUT IT!"

"DON'T MAKE SUCH A BIG DEAL OUT OF YOUR
FIRST DAY BACK TO SCHOOL!"

"THE ONE NAMED HEATHCLIFF HAS ESCAPED!"

"EVEN WHEN YOU CATCH HIM RED HANDED, HE HAS THAT CERTAIN SAVOIR-FAIRE!"

"HEATHCLIFF GOT A FREE WHISTLE IN THIS BOX OF CAT YUMMIES."

"LET ME KNOW IF HE BOTHERS YOU."

"WHY, THANK YOU!"

"WHAT'LL WE CALL IT, GRANDPA?"

"CAN'T YOU *EVER* RESIST DUMPING A GARBAGE CAN?!"

"WE GOT SAND IN HIS TUNA FISH."

"OH, HOW NICE !... YOUR DOLLY IS WALKING !..."

"MINE CAN EVEN RUN !"

"HEATHCLIFF IS SIGNALING FOR A CURVE."

"ANYONE FOR ICE CREAM?"

"REMEMBER, NEVER TAKE WORMS FROM STRANGERS!"

"HEATHCLIFF'S FOUND A SALE ON CAT FOOD!"

"HE'S DOING 'CAT ON A HOT TIN ROOF'."

"I THINK YOU'VE PUNISHED THEM LONG ENOUGH...
YOU SHOULD RETURN TO YOUR FAMILY."

"THAT LITTLE GUY!... HE BOUGHT A CAN OF MINNOWS AND THEN HE ATE THEM!!"

"OH-OH!...OL' SPIKE'S REALLY IN FOR IT *THIS* TIME!"

"WELL, HIS PROBLEM CERTAINLY ISN'T MALNUTRITION!"

"I CAN'T FIND THAT LARGE LOAF OF ITALIAN BREAD!"

"OH, DEAR!...WE FORGOT TO BRING HEATHCLIFF'S BIKINI!"

"IT'S BEEN TAKEN CARE OF."

"YOU'RE A BIG HELP!"

"PACKAGE FOR HEATHCLIFF NUTMEG.
...SIGN HERE, PLEASE."

"HE'S IN HERE, GRANDMA...WATCHING YOGA EXERCISES."

"OH, OH!"

"YOU GOT THREE MICE IN JANUARY, DOWN TWO
IN FEBRUARY, UP AGAIN IN MARCH..."

"OH BROTHER!...WHAT HAVE YOU GUYS BEEN UP TO?!"

"IT'S THE ONLY WAY I CAN GET HIM TO COME!"

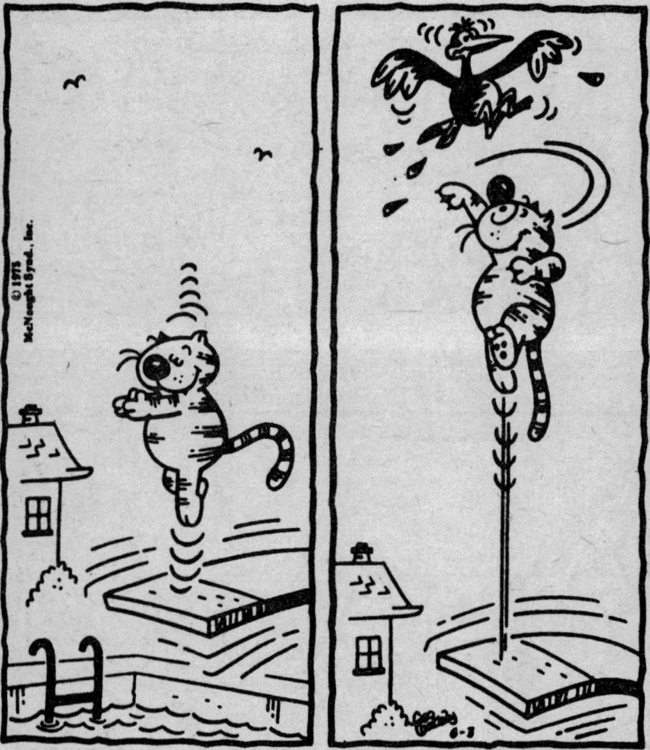

© 1975
McNaught Synd., Inc.
6-3

"ORDINARILY, HIS MILKMAN TRAPS AREN'T THIS ELABORATE!"

"I COULD HAVE SWORN I SAW
HEATHCLIFF SWIPE A FISH!"

"IT SAYS HERE THEY'RE DESIGNING A NEW CLOCK FOR THE TOWN HALL STEEPLE."

"GRANDMA, WOULD YOU CHECK THE TEA POT?...
HEATHCLIFF'S LIZARD GOT AWAY."

"WELL, I SUPPOSE WE SHOULD BE GOING."

"HERE GRANDPA...HEATHCLIFF AND ME FIXED YOU BREAKFAST IN BED!"

"WE'RE ONLY BOARDING HEATHCLIFF OUT OVERNIGHT!!"

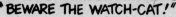
"BEWARE THE WATCH-CAT!"

" FEET UP, DEAR. "

"IF THE PRICE OF THE CAT FOOD HAS GONE UP AGAIN, DUCK!"

"VERY GOOD!...VERY GOOD INDEED!"

"OH, DEAR!...I JUST CAN'T REMEMBER... WHAT IS THAT
CATFOOD HEATHCLIFF IS SO FOND OF ?!"

"JUST A PLEASANT SMILE WILL BE SUFFICIENT, HEATHCLIFF."

"YOU CAN CHECK FOR CAT FOOD COUPONS
WHEN I'VE FINISHED THE PAPER!"

10-5

1977
McNaught Synd., Inc.

" YOU AGAIN ?! "

"OH, DEAR!...SOMEONE IS A SORE LOSER!!"

"GETTING ALL SET FOR THE WORLD SERIES OPENER?"

"ANYTIME YOU'RE READY."

"THE DOG CATCHER NEARLY GOT CHAUNCY!"